만공 선사 법훈

(滿空禪師 法訓)

만공 선사 법훈

초판 인쇄: 2025년 11월 20일
감수/발행: 선승 무초 (禪僧 無超)
발행처: 도서출판 지장원(地藏院)
등록: 420-2021-000001(2021년 01월 06일)
주소: 강원도 강릉시 연곡면 수터골길 171
전화: 010-4668-5108
이메일: tothezen@gmail.com
정가: 10,000원
ISBN: 979-11-973493-5-5 (03220)

Seon Master Mangong's Dharma Talks

First Edition Printed: November 20, 2025
Supervised and Published by: Seon Monk Mucho
Publisher: Jijangwon
Registration No.: 420-2021-000001 (January 6, 2021)
Address: 171 Suteogol-gil, Yeongok-myeon, Gangneung-si, Gangwon-do, Korea
Phone: +82-10-4668-5108
Email: tothezen@gmail.com
Price: USD $8.00
ISBN: 979-11-973493-5-5 (03220)

서 언

불교란 무엇인가? 불교란 어떤 가르침을 전하고 있는가? 라는 물음에 이 책은 명쾌한 답변을 전해줍니다. 이『만공 선사 법훈』은 근세의 선지식이었던 만공 선사(1872~1946)의 법문으로 그 내용이 길지는 않지만 촌철살인의 선지(禪旨)로 불가(佛家)에서 특히 선가(禪家)에서는 널리 읽히고 있는 글입니다. 이 간명하면서도 고준한 선사의 가르침을 잘 읽고, 마음에 새겨서, 자유(깨달음)의 길로 가는 인연이 되시기를 바랍니다.

이 책은 2021년 출간된 한글『만공선사법훈』과 영문『Seon Master Man Gong's Dharma Talks』의 두 책을 수정 보완하여 한권으로 묶은 것입니다. 이전의 영역본과는 차이가 있습니다. 요즘 더 많은 국내·국외 사람들이 절을 찾고, 불교의 지혜란 무엇인지를 묻고 있습니다. 더욱이 더 많은 외국인분들이 한국어를 배우고, 불교를 배우고자 합니다. 이 책을 읽으신 한국 분들은 주위의 외국인 분들이나, 해외의 외국인 분들에게 일독(一讀)을 권해주시기 바랍니다.

무초 합장

불교는 자아를 완성하는 길이며
완벽한 철학이다.

● 목 차 ●

● 1. 나를 찾아야 할 필요와 나 ●

1. 사람이 만물 가운데 가장 귀하다는 뜻은 '나'를 찾아 얻는 데 있나 니라.

2. '나'라는 의의가 절대자유(絶對自由)로움에 있는 것으로 모든 것은 내 마음대로 자재(自在)할 수 있어야 할 것임에도 불구하고 우리 인간은 어느 때, 어느 곳에도 자유가 없고, 무엇 하나 임의(任意)로 되지 않는 것은 망아(妄我)가 주인이 되고 진아(眞我)가 종이 되어 살아 나가는 까닭이니라.

3. 망아는 진아의 소생(所生)인데 현재 우리가 쓰고 있는 마음은 곧 사심(邪心)이요, 진아는 정심(正心)으로 시종(始終)도 없고, 존망(存亡)도 없고, 형상(形象)도 없지마는 오히려 조금도 부족함이 없는 '나'이니라.

4. 사람이 나를 잊어버린 바에야 육축(六畜)[1]으로 동류(同類) 되는 인간이라 아니 할 수 없나니, 짐승이 본능적으로 식색(食色)[2]에만 팔려서 허둥거리는 것이나, 제 진면목(眞面目)이 무엇인지도 모르고 현실에만 끌려서 헤매는 것이나, 무엇이 다를 것인가? 세상에서 아무리 위대하다는 인물이라고 하더라도 자기면목(自己面目)을 모른다면 사생육취(四生六趣)[3]에 윤회하는 한 분자(分子)에 지나지 아니 하나니라.

5. 동업중생(同業衆生)이 사는 이 사바세계(娑婆世界)에는 너

---

1) 집에서 기르는 대표적인 여섯 가축. 소, 말, 돼지, 양, 닭, 개
2) 식욕(食慾)과 색욕(色慾)
3) 사생은 생물이 생겨나는 네 가지 형식으로 태생(胎生), 난생(卵生), 습생(濕生), 화생(化生)이고, 육취는 중생이 업인(業因)에 따라 가게 되는 지옥·아귀·축생·아수라·인간·천상의 여섯 곳.

와 내가 다 같은 생활을 하기 때문에 사람 사는 것이 그저 그렇거니 하고 무심히 살며, 자기들 앞에 가로 놓인 무서운 일을 예측하지 못하고 그럭저럭 살다가 죽음에 닥치면 앞길이 망망하게 되나 니라.

6. '나' 라고 하는 것은 '아무개야!' 하고 부르면 '네' 하고 대답하는 바로 그것인데, 그것은 생사도 없고, 불에 타거나, 물에 젖거나, 칼에 상하는 것이 아니어서 일체 얽매임을 떠난 독립적인 '나' 이다.

7. 인생은 말꼬리에 매달려 울며 뒹굴려 가는 죄수처럼 업(業)의 사슬에 끌려 생로병사의 고(苦)의 길을 영겁(永劫)으로 순력(巡歷)하고 있는데, 그 쇠사슬은 자기의 지혜 칼이라야 능히 끊어 버릴 수 있게 되나 니라.

8. 사회에서 뛰어난 학식과 인격으로 존경받는 아무러한 사람이라도 이 일[4]을 알지 못하면 기실 사람의 정신은 잃어버린 인간이니라.

9. 석가세존(釋迦世尊)이 탄생 시 산석(産席)에서 한 손으로 하늘을 가리키고 또 한 손으로 땅을 가리키며 "천상천하(天上天下) 유아독존(唯我獨尊)" 이라 하신 그 '아(我)'도 나를 가리킨 것이니라.

10. 각자가 다 부처가 될 성품은 지니었지만, 내가 나를 알지 못하기 때문에 부처를 이루지 못 하나니라.

11. 일체가 다 '나'이기 때문에 극히 작은 하나의 털끝만한 정력이라도 이 '나'를 찾는 이외의 어떤 다른 것에 소모하는

---

4) 나를 찾는 일

것은 나의 손실이니라.

12. 누구든지 육신(肉身), 업신(業身), 법신(法身) 세 몸을 지녔는데, 세 몸이 일체가 되어 하나로 쓰는 때라야 올바른 사람이 되는 것이니라.

13. 일체 행동은 법신이 하는 것이나, 육신과 업신을 떠난 법신이 아닌 까닭에 현상(現像) 그대로가 곧 생사 없는 법신의 자리이니라.

14. 생사 없는 그 자리는 유정물(有情物)이나 무정물(無情物)이 다 지녔기 때문에 한 가닥 풀의 정(情)이라도 전 우주의 무장(武裝)으로도 해체(解體)시킬 수 없나 니라.

15. 세상에는 나를 알아보느니 찾아보느니 하는 말과 문구(文句)는 있으나, 업식(業識)으로 아는 나를 생각할 뿐이요, 정말 나는 어떤 것인지 상상조차 하지 못 하나니라.

16. 나는 무한 극수적(無限 極數的) 수명(壽命)을 가진 것으로, 죽을 레야 죽을 수 없는 금강불괴신(金剛 不壞身)[5]이라 이 육체의 생사는 나의 옷을 바꾸어 입는 것일 뿐, 인간이라면 자신이 소유한 생사의 옷쯤은 자유자재로 벗고 입을 줄 알아야 되나 니라.

17. 보고 들어서 얻는 지식으로서는 얻을 수 없는 것이니라. '나'라는 생각만 해도 그것은 벌써 내가 아니니라.

18. 나는 무념처(無念處)[6]에서 찾을 수 있는 것이니, 그것은

---

5) 금강과 같이 견고하여 괴멸되지 않는 몸. 곧 불신(佛身).
6) 무아(無我)의 경지에 이르러 아무 생각이 없는 곳.

무념처에 일체유(一切有)가 갖추어져 있기 때문이다.

19. 부처를 대상으로 하여 구경(究竟)[7]에 이르면 내가 곧 부처인 것이 발견되나니, 결국 내가 나 안에서 나를 발견해야 하나니라.

---

7) 사리(事理)의 마지막.

● 2. 나를 찾는 법 ― 참선법 ●

1. 세상에는 나를 찾는 법을 가르쳐 주는 선생도 없고, 장소도 없고, 다만 불교 안에 있는 선방(禪房)에서만 나를 찾는 유일한 정로(正路)를 가르쳐 주나 니라.

2. 수도(修道: 參禪)한다는 것은 각자가 자기 정신을 수습해 가는 그 공부를 한다는 말인데, 누구에게나 다 시급한 일이 아닐 수 없나 니라.

3. 세상의 학문은 단지 그 몸의 망상에서 일시의 이용으로 끝나고 말지만, 참선학(參禪學)은 세세생생(世世生生)에 어떤 때, 어떤 곳, 어떤 몸으로, 어떤 생활을 하든지 구애됨이 없이 활용되는 학문이니라.

4. 선방만 선방이 아니라 참선하는 사람은 각각 자기 육체가 곧 선방이라. 선방에 상주(常住)하는 것이 행주좌와(行住坐臥) 어묵동정(語默動靜)에 간단(間斷)없이 정진할 수 있나 니라.

5. 참선은 절대로 혼자는 하지 못하는 것이니, 반드시 선지식(善知識)을 여의지 말아야 하나니, 선지식은 인생 문제를 비롯하여 일체 문제에 걸림이 없이 바르게 가르쳐 주나 니라.

6. 선지식을 만나 법문 한마디 얻어 듣기란 천만겁에 만나기 어려운 일이니, 법문 한 마디를 옳게 알아듣는다면 참선할 것이 없이 곧 나를 깨달을 수 있나 니라.

7. 법문 들을 때는 엷은 얼음 밟듯 정신을 모아 간절한 마음으로 들어야 하나니라.

8. 선지식은 선생이니 박사니 하는 막연한 이름뿐이 아니라, 일체 이치에 요달(了達)된 사람으로 불조(佛祖)의 혜명(慧命)을 상속(相續)받은 분이니라.

9. 이(理)와 사(事)는 같은 원(圓)이라, 어느 각도에서 출발하든지 쉬지 않고 걸어가면 그 목적이 이루어질 수 있기는 하지만, 나를 발견 [자각(自覺)]하기까지는 선지식의 가르침이 없이는 될 수 없나 니라.

10. 선지식의 법문을 듣고도 흘려버리고 하여, 신행(信行)이 없으면 법문을 다시 듣지 못하는 과보(果報)를 얻나 니라.

11. 선지식을 믿는 그 정도에 따라 자신의 공부가 성취되나 니라.

12. 장맛이 짠 줄을 아는 사람은 다 공부할 수 있나 니라.

13. 공부가 잘 되지 않는 것은 전생(前生)에 놀고 지낸 탓이니, 그 빚을 어서 갚아야 수입이 있게 되나 니라.

14. 남음 없는 신심(信心)만 있으면 도의 기반은 이미 튼튼해진 것이니라.

15. 신심(信心), 분심(憤心), 의심(疑心) 세 마음을 합하여야 공부를 성취할 수 있나 니라.

16. 신심만 철저하면 나의 정기(定氣)에 대상을 곧 정당화시켜서 자율적 성취가 있게 되나 니라.

17. 법문을 듣고도 신심이 동(動)하지 않는 인간이라면 내세

(來世)에는 다시 인간의 몸을 받기가 어려우니라.

18. 공부하는 사람이 제일 주의해야 할 것은 먼저 나를 가르쳐 줄 선지식을 택하여야 하고, 나를 완성한 후에 남을 지도할 생각을 해야 하나 니라.

19. 명안종사(明眼宗師)의 인가(印可)도 없이 자칭 선지식으로 남을 가르치는 죄가 가장 크니라.

20. 이 법은 언어가 끊어지고 심행처(心行處)가 멸한 곳(언어도단 심행처멸: 언어의 길이 끊기고 마음 작용이 멈춤)에서 발견되는 도리라, 다만 마음과 마음이 서로 응답(應答)하여 상속하는 법으로, 선지식의 직접 가르침이 아니면 배울 수 없는 도리니라.

21. 공부는 발심[發心: 보리심 (깨닫고자 하는 마음)을 일으킴] 본위라 별로 제한 받을 것은 없으나, 학령(學齡)으로는 이십(二十)세로부터 삼십(三十)세 까지가 적령(適齡)이니라.

22. 참선법은 평범한 연구나 공부가 아니요, (상)대(對)가 끊어진 참구법(參究法) 곧 터럭 하나 얼씬거리지 못하는 경지에 이르러야 하나니라.

23. 백년의 연구가 일분간의 무념처(無念處)에서 얻은 한낱 이것만 같지 못하다.

24. 일체 중생은 날 때부터 이성(異性)의 감응(感應)으로 말미암아 세세생생에 익히는 것이 음양(陰陽)법이니, 정신을 모으는데 있어, 이성적(異性的) 장애가 제일 힘이 센 것이니, 공부하는 사람은 이성(異性)을 가장 멀리 해야 하나니라.

25. 일체 생각을 쉬고 일념(一念)에 들되, 일념이라는 생각조차 잊어버린 무념처에서 한 걸음 더 나아가야 나를 발견하나니라.

26. 소아(小兒)적 나는 소멸되어야 하기 때문에 공부의 성취를 하기 전에는 썩은 그루터기같이 되어 추호도 돌아보지 않을 만큼 나의 존재를 없애야 하나니라.

27. 나를 완성시키는 데는 삼대(三大) 조건이 구비되어야 하는데, 그것은 도량(道場), 도사(道師), 도반(道伴)이니라.

28. 도를 지키는 사람은 도절(道節)을 지켜야 하는 것이니, 도는 하나이다. 도를 가르치는 방법은 조금씩 다르기 때문에 도절을 지키지 않으면 정신적으로 시간적으로 손실을 보게 되느니라.

29. 짚신 한 켤레를 삼는 데도 선생이 있고, 이름 있는 버섯한 송이도 나는 땅이 있는데, 일체 만물을 총섭(總攝)하는 도를 알려는 사람이 도인의 가르침 없이 어찌 도인이 될 수 있으며, 천하정기(天下正氣)를 다 모아 차지한 도인이 나는 땅이 어찌 특별히 있지 않을 것인가. 그리고 도반(道伴)의 감화력은 선생의 가르침보다도 강한 것이니라.

30. 참선을 하여 인생 문제만 해결되면 억생(億生) 억겁(億劫)에 지은 갖은 악, 갖은 죄가 다 소멸되나니, 그 때는 사생육취(四生六趣)에 헤메는 고생을 다시는 받지 않게 되나 니라.

31. 수도(修道) 중에는 사람 노릇할 것은 아주 단념해 버리고 귀먹고 눈먼 병신이 되어, 일체 다른 일에 간섭이 없게 되면 대아(大我)는 저절로 이루어지나 니라.

32. 참선법은 상래(上來)로 있는 것이지만, 중간에 선지식들이 화두(話頭)드는 법으로 참선하는 법을 가르치기 시작하여 그 후로 무수(無數) 도인(道人)이 출현하였나니, 화두는 천칠백(千七百) 공안(公案)[8]이나 있는데, 내가 처음 들던 화두는 곧 "만법귀일(萬法歸一) 일귀하처(一歸何處) : 모든 것은 하나로 돌아가는데 그 하나는 어디로 돌아가는가?"를 의심하였는데, 이 화두는 이중적 의심이라 처음 배우는 사람은 '만법은 하나로 돌아갔다고 하니, 그 하나는 무엇인고?'하고 의심하여 가되 의심한다는 생각까지 끊어진 적적(寂寂)하고 성성(惺惺)한 무념처에 들어가야 나를 볼 수 있게 되나 니라.

33. 하나(一)라는 것은 있는 것도 아니요, 없는 것도 아니요, 이 정신도 영혼도 아니요, 마음도 아니니, 하나라는 것은 과연 무엇인고? 의심을 지어 가되 고양이가 쥐를 노릴 때에 일념에 들 듯, 물이 흘러갈 때에 간단(間斷)이 없듯, 의심을 간절히 하여 가면 반드시 하나를 알게 되나 니라.

34. 참선한다고 하면서 조금이라도 다른 데 미련이 남아 있거나, 인간으로서의 자랑거리인 학문이나, 기이한 재주 등 무엇이라도 남은 미련이 있다면 참선하기는 어려운 사람인 것이니, 아주 백지로 돌아가야 하나니라.

35. 크게 나의 구속(拘束)에 단련을 치른다면 그 대가로 큰 나의 자유를 얻게 되나 니라.

36. 예전에는 선지식의 일언지하(一言之下)에 돈망(頓忘)생사(生死)하는 이도 있고, 늦어야 삼(三)일, 칠(七)일에 견성(見性)[9]한 이도 많다는데, 지금 사람들은 근기(根機)도 빈약하지

---

8) 선(禪)에서 도를 깨치기 위하여 참구하는 화두(話頭). 한 사람의 사안(私案)이 아니고 조사(祖師)들의 정안결택(正眼決擇).

만 참선을 부업(副業)으로 해 가기 때문에 이십(二十)년, 삼십년 공부한 사람이 불법(佛法)의 대의(大義)를 모르는 이가 거의 전부니라.

37. 밥을 자기가 먹어야 배가 부른 것과 같이, 참선도 제가 하지 않으면 부처님도 선지식도 제도해 주지 못 하나니라.

38. 참선하려면 먼저 육국(六國)[10] 전란(戰亂)을 평정시켜 마음이 안정되어야 비로소 공부할 준비가 된 것이니라.

39. 가장 자유롭고 제일 간편한 공부이기 때문에 이 공부를 할 줄 아는 사람은 염라국(閻羅國) 차사(差使)의 눈도 피할 수 있나 니라.

40. 한 생각이 일어날 때 일체가 생기고, 한 생각이 멸할 때 일체가 멸하나 니라. 내 한 생각의 기멸(起滅)이 곧 우주의 건괴(建壞)요 인생의 생사니라.

41. 말이 입에서 나오기 전에 그르쳤다 함은 물질 이전의 마음을 지적한 것이니라.

42. 공부가 잘 된다고 느낄 때 공부와는 벌써 어긋난 것이니라.

43. 꿈속에서 공부해 가는 것을 증험(證驗)하여 선생으로 삼을 것이니라.

---

9) 모든 망혹(妄惑)을 버리고 자기의 심성(心性)을 사무쳐 알고, 모든 법의 실상인 당체(當體)와 일치하는 정각(正覺)을 이룸.
10) 眼耳鼻舌身意; 눈, 귀, 코, 혀, 몸, 뜻

44. 꿈도 없고 생사도 없이 잠이 푹 들었을 때에 안심입명처(安心立命處)를 어디에 두는지 알아야 하나니라.

45. 꿈이라 하는 것은 업신(業身)[11]의 동작인데, 깨어 있을 때는 생각만으로 헤매다가 잘 때 업신이 제 몸을 나투어 가지고 육신이 하던 행동을 짓는 것이니라.

46. 꿈과 생시[몽각(夢覺)][12]가 일여(一如)하게 공부를 해 나아갈 수 있어야 하나니라.

47. 산몸이 불에 탈 때에도 정상적 정신을 가질 수 있겠나? 헤아려서 미치지 못한다면 사선(死線)을 넘을 때 자기 전로(前路)가 막막하게 될 것을 알아야 하느니라.

48. 공부인(工夫人)이 공부를 아니 하는 공부를 하여야 하는데, 공부 아니 하기가 하기보다 더욱 어려우니라.

49. 공부를 잘하고 못하는 문제보다도 이 공부밖에 할 일이 없다는 결정적 신심(信心)부터 세워야 하나니라.

50. 깨닫기 전(悟前)이나 깨달은 후(오후, 悟後)나 한 번씩 죽을 고비를 넘겨야 하나니라.

51. 참선은 모든 업장(業障)[13]과 습기(習氣)를 녹이는 도가니(옹, 甕)니라.

52. 사람을 대할 때에는 자비심(慈悲心)으로 대하여야 하지

---

11) 영혼
12) 꿈과 생시
13) 전생에 지은 허물로 인하여 이승에서 받는 마장(魔障).

만, 공부를 위하여서는 극악(極惡)극독(劇毒)심이 아니면 팔만사천(八萬四千) 번뇌마(煩惱魔)[14]를 쳐부수지 못 하나니라.

53. 사형이 집행될 시간 직전에도 오히려 여념(餘念)이 있을지 모르지만, 정진(精進)중에는 털끝만한 어른거림이라도 섞여서는 아니 되나 니라.

54. 공부하는 데는 망상보다도 수마(睡魔)가 두려운 것이니, 수마를 먼저 조복(調伏)시켜야 하나니라.

55. 인신(人身)을 얻기가 극히 어려운 일이니 사람 몸 가졌을 이 때를 놓치지 말고 공부에 힘쓰라. 사람 몸 한번 놓치게 되면 또 다시 만나기 어려울 것이니라.

56. 공부에 득력(得力)을 못하였을 때 안광낙지(眼光落地)하게 되면 인업(人業)만 남아 짐승도 미남미녀로 보여서 그 뱃속에 들기 쉬우니라.

57. 참선하는 사람의 시간은 지극히 귀중한 것이라, 촌음(寸陰)을 허비하지 말아야 하느니라.

58. 변소에 앉아 있는 동안처럼 자유롭고 한가한 시간이 없나니, 그 때만이라도 일념에 든다면 견성(見性)할 수 있나 니라.

59. 공부가 늦어지는 까닭은 시간 여유가 있거니 하고 항상 미루는 마음이 있기 때문이니라. 자고 나면 오늘도 죽지 않

---

14) 사마(四魔)의 하나: 노여움(진에瞋恚), 지나친 욕심(탐욕貪慾), 어리석고 못남(우치愚癡), 번뇌(煩惱) 등 사마(四魔)가 사람을 괴롭히고 어지럽게 하여 불도 수행에 방해가 됨.

고 살았으니, 살아있는 오늘에 공부를 마쳐야 하지 내일을 어찌 믿으랴! 하고 매일매일 스스로 격려해 가야 하나니라.

60. 밤 자리에 누울 때 하루 동안의 공부를 점검하여 망상과 졸음으로 정진 시간보다 많이 하였거든 다시 큰 용기를 내어 정진하되, 매일매일 한결같이 할 것이니라.

61. 공부하다가 졸리거나 망상이 나거든 생사 대사(大事)에 자유롭지 못한 자신의 전정(前程)을 다시 살펴본다면 정신이 저절로 새로워 질 것이니라.

62. 사선을 넘을 때 털끝만큼이라도 사심(私心)의 여유가 있다면 참선하는 기억조차 사라져 없어지느니라.

63. 생사윤회의 생활을 면하려고 출가하여 스님이 되었으니 참선법을 여의고 하는 일은 모두가 생사법(生死法)을 익히는 것이니라.

64. 도(道)라는 것이 따로 있는 줄 알고 구하는 마음으로 참선한다면 외도(外道)에 떨어지게 되나 니라.

65. 설사 도인이 온갖 신통변화를 부리고 죽을 때에도 불가사의(不可思議)한 이적(異蹟)을 보일지라도 이는 상법(相法)이니, 이런 상법이란 하나도 가히 취할 바는 아니니라.

66. 믿음은 부처를 찾아 오르는 발판이기 때문에 몰아(沒我) 적 믿음의 발판을 딛고 부처를 넘어 각자의 자기 정체(正體)를 찾아야 하나니라.

67. 선학자(禪學者)는 선학자의 행위를 엄숙히 가져서 입을

열지 않고서라도 남을 가르치게 되어야 하나니라.

68. 공부의 과정(課程)에는 지무생사(知無生死)[15], 계무생사(契無生死)[16], 체무생사(體無生死)[17], 용무생사(用無生死)[18]의 네 가지 단계가 있는데, 용무생사에 이르러야 비로소 이무애(理無碍)[19] 사무애(事無碍)[20] 하게 되는 대자유인(大自由人)이 되나 니라.

69. 공부할 때에 짐짓 알려는 생각을 말고, 정진력만 얻으면 공부는 저절로 성취되나 니라.

70. 공부가 완성되기 전에 미리 알았다는 생각을 가지고 게을리 하다가는 불법인연(佛法因緣)마저 떨어지기 쉬우니라.

71. 물체에 의존하지 아니하는 정신은 한 모양도 없는 자리에서 일체 행동으로 능히 현실화할 수 있나 니라.

72. 정신은 물질의 창조자이지만, 물질이 아니면 정신의 존재와 효과가 나타나지 못하나 니라.

73. 물질은 각자 그 이름에 따르는 한 가지 책임을 할 뿐인데, 정신은 이름도 형상도 없지만 만유(萬有)의 근본(바탕)이라, 어디서 무슨 일에나 절대 능력자이니, 이 정신은 누구나 다 가지고 있다. 이 정신만 도로 찾으면 만능(萬能)의 인(人)이 되나 니라.

---

15) 지무생사; 생사없음을 아는 것.
16) 계무생사; 생사 없는 경지에 계합하는 것.
17) 체무생사; 생사 없는 경지를 체달함.
18) 용무생사; 생사 없는 경지를 내 마음대로 수용(需用)하는 것.
19) 이치(理致)에 걸림이 없는 지무생사, 계무생사의 경지.
20) 사물(事物)에 걸림이 없는 체무생사, 용무생사의 경지.

74. 정신이라는 전당(殿堂) 안에는 생사와 선악이라는 두 배우가 순번(順番)으로 삼라만상(森羅萬象)이란 배경 앞에서 희비극을 무한한 형태(形態)로 연출하고 있나 니라.

75. 아무리 문명이 발달한 나라라 하더라도 도인이 없으면 빈 나라요, 아무리 빈약한 나라라 하더라도 도인이 한 사람이라도 있으면 그 나라는 비지 않은 나라이니라.

76. 도인(道人)은 도인이라는 대명사(代名詞)에 지나지 않는 도인이 되어서는 안 된다. 명상(名相)이 생기기 이전 소식을 증득(證得)하여, 도인이라는 우상(偶像)도 여의고, 계(戒)니 수행(修行)이니 하는 구속에서 벗어나 완전 독립적 인간이 되어야 육도에 순력(巡歷)하면서 고(苦)를 면하게 되나 니라.

● 3. 현세 인생(現世 人生)에 대하여 ●

1. 인간의 일생은 짧은 한 막의 연극에 지나지 않는데, 이 연극의 한 장면이 종막이 되면 희노애락(喜怒哀樂)을 연출하던 그 의식은 그만 자취 없이 사라져 버리고 육체는 부글부글 썩어 버리니, 이 얼마나 허망한 일인가? 이 허망하기 짝이 없는 그 동안인들 일(一)분의 자유가 있었던가? 밥을 먹다가도 불의(不意)의 죽음이 닥치면 씹던 밥도 못 삼키고 죽어야 하고, 집을 아무리 많은 돈을 들여 찬란하게 짓다가도 느닷없이 화재(火災)라도 만나면 방 안에 한 번 앉아 보지도 못하고 허망하게 되지 않는가? 직접 내 자신의 일에도 이렇게 늘 자유를 잃어버리는데 인생의 집단인 사회와 국가를 세운다는 일이 얼마나 서글픈 일인가? 자유의 바탕을 얻어야 근본적 자유를 얻게 될 것이 아닌가. 자유가 어디에서 얻어지는지도 모르는 인간들이 자유를 부르짖는 것은, 쌀도 없이 밥을 지어 배부르게 먹는 이야기만으로 떠드는 셈이니라.

2. 인생은 자기업신(自己業身)의 반영(反映)인 몽환(夢幻) 세계를 실상(實相)으로 알고 울고 웃고 하는 것은 마치 은행나무가 물에 비치는 제 그림자를 이성(異性)으로 감응(感應)하여 열매를 맺는 것과 같으니라.

3. 인간이 산다는 것은 생의 연속이 아니라, 생멸(生滅)의 연속으로 인간이 죽는 순간도 죽기 전후 생활도 다 잊어버리고, 입태(入胎)[21] 출태(出胎)[22]의 고(苦)도 기억하지 못하고, 다만 현실적 육식(六識)[23]으로 판단할 수 있는 이 생활만 느끼

---

21) 어머니 복중(腹中)에 잉태(孕胎)됨을 말함.
22) 어머니에게서 세상에 태어남.
23) 안식(眼識), 이식(耳識), 비식(鼻識), 설식(舌識), 신식(身識), 의식(意識).

고 사는데, 천당에 갔다가 지옥에 갔다가 사람이 되었다가 짐승으로 떨어졌다가 하는 그러한 생이 금세 지나가고, 또 한 생이 금세 닥쳐오는 것이 마치 활동사진의 영상(影像)이 연속해 교환 이동되어 빠른 찰나에 다른 장면으로 나타나는 것과 같으니라.

4. 인생은 과거를 부를 수도 없고, 미래를 보증할 수도 없는 것이다. 현재가 현재이기 때문에 현재를 완전히 파악하게 되어야 과거 현재 미래의 생활을 일단화(一單化)한 생활을 할 수 있나 니라.

5. 인생은 과거에 사는 것도 아니요, 미래에 사는 것도 아니요, 다만 현재에만 살고 있는데, 현재란 잠시도 머무름이 없이 과거에서 미래로 이동하는 순간이니, 그 순간에 느끼는 불안정한 삶을 어찌 실(實)답다 할 수 있으랴! 과거와 현재가 합치된 현실이 있나니 현재는 과거의 후신(後身)이요, 미래의 전신(前身)으로 과거—현재—미래가 하나이기 때문이다.

6. 우리가 사는 세계를 중심으로 하여 위로 상상할 수 없는 최고 문화세계가 헤아릴 수 없이 벌어져 있고, 아래로 저열(低劣) 극악(極惡)한 그 양과 수를 헤일 수 없는 지옥의 세계가 다 함께 몽환세계(夢幻世界)[24]인 것이니, 과연 어떤 것이 실세계(實世界)인지? 그것을 알아 얻는 것이 곧 진아(眞我)세계를 체달[25]하게 되는 것이니라.

7. 나의 현재 생활이 일체(一切)세계라, 현재 생활에서 자족(自足)을 못 얻으면 다시 얻을 도리가 없나 니라.

---

24) 꿈과 환상처럼 덧없는 세계.
25) 사물의 진상을 몸소 통달함.

8. 인간들은 모두 자기에게는 좋은 것이 와야 할 희망을 갖고 생을 이어 가지만 좋은 것을 취하는 것이 곧 언짢은 것을 얻는 원인인 줄을 알지 못하나 니라.

9. 인간 생활의 주체(主體)가 되는 생로병사(生老病死)와 희로애락(喜怒哀樂)까지도 다생(多生)으로 익혀 온 망령된 습관의 취집(聚集)이요 결과임을 확실히 깨달아야 생사를 벗어나게 되나 니라.

10. 이 우주에는 무한(無限) 극수(極數)적 이류(異類)중생이 꽉 차서 자기 습성에 맞는 생활권을 건립하고 있지만, 우리 육식(六識)은 다생(多生)의 습기(習氣)로 점점 고정화(固定化)하여 우리 사바세계 인간으로는 어느 정도 한도를 넘어서는 도저히 볼 수 없고, 느낄 수도 없나니, 천인(天人)이니 지옥이니 신(神)이니 귀(鬼)니 하는 것도 결국 우리 육식(六識)으로는 판단할 수 없는 이류 중생의 명상(名相)이니라.

11. 습관은 천성이라 천재(天才)니 소질(素質)이니 하는 것도 다생으로 많이 익혀서 고정화하여 이루어진 것인데, 이것이 바로 업(業)이라는 것이다.

12. 물체는 결합(結合) 해소(解消)의 이중(二重)작용(作用)을 하기 때문에 영겁을 두고 우주는 건괴(建壞)되고, 인생은 생사를 반복하고 있나 니라.

13. 중생이라 하는 것은 한 개체에 국한된 소아(小我)적인 생활을 하는 사람 짐승 벌레 등으로 일체 자유를 잃어버리게 되어 다만 업풍(業風)에 불려서 사생(四生)육취(六趣)에 헤매게 되는 것이요, 불[佛, 완인(完人)]이라 하는 것은 일체 우주를 자신화(自身化)하여 일체 중생이 다 내 한 몸이요 삼천대

천세계(三千大千世界)[26]가 다 내 한 집이라, 어느 집이나 어느 몸이나 취하고 버리는 것을 내 임의로 하나니라.

14. 완인(完人)은 만유(萬有)를 자체화(自體化)하였기 때문에 만유의 형상을 임의로 지으며, 만유의 도리를 자유로 쓰게 되나 니라.

15. (중생은) 천당은 갈 곳이요, 지옥은 못 갈 곳이라 한다; 우주가 내 한 몸이요, 천당과 지옥이 내 한 집인데, 중생은 한 세계를 두 세계로 갈라놓고, 한 몸을 분신(分身)시켜 천당 지옥으로 나누어 보내는데, 이것은 중생의 업연으로 됨이니라.

16. 인격(人格)이 환경에 휘둘리는 사람은 영원한 평안(平安)을 얻을 길이 없나 니라.

17. 세상 사람들은 똥과 피의 주머니로 몸을 삼고 춥고 덥고 목마르고 배고픈 것만 귀중히 여기기 때문에 길이 윤회(輪廻)의 고취(苦趣)를 면치 못 하나니라.

18. 우리가 느끼는 안이비설신의(眼耳鼻舌身意)의 여섯 가지 식(識: 眼識, 耳識, 鼻識, 舌識, 身識, 意識)은 장소에 따라 변하고 때에 따라 흩어지나니, 이렇게 시시각각으로 천류(遷流)하는 여섯 가지 식(識)으로 어찌 인생이 근본정신을 파악할 수 있겠는가?

19. 세인(世人)들의 아무리 진보된 이론이나 심원(深遠)한 학

---

26) 수미산을 중심으로 하여 해, 달, 사대주(四大洲), 육욕천(六欲天), 범천(梵天) 등을 합하여 한 세계라 하고, 이것을 천 배 한 것을 소천(小千)세계, 소천 세계를 천 배 한 것을 중천(中千)세계, 중천 세계를 천 배 한 것을 대천 세계라 하는데, 이것들의 전부를 말함.

설(學說)이라 할지라도 그것으로는 인생 문제를 도저히 해결할 수 없는 것이니 이는 명상(名相)에 집착되었기 때문이니라.

20. 이론으로는 해결할 수 없는 것을 명확하게 깨우쳐 주는 이론이라면, 그 이론은 곧 도의 입문으로 인도하는 대도사(大導師)가 되는 것이니라.

21. 형이상학(形而上學)이나 유심론(唯心論)을 말하는 자 스스로 물질적 영역을 벗어나지 못한 것을 모르 나니라.

22. 세상에는 바른 말 하는 사람도 없는 동시에 그른 말을 하는 사람도 있지 않은 것이니라.

23. 신(神)은 아무리 신통(神通)자재(自在)한 최고신으로 인류의 화복(禍福)을 주재(主宰)한다 하더라도 육체를 갖추지 못한 사(邪)이니라.

24. 신의 존재를 부인하는 사람은 무지(無知)를 면치 못하고, 신을 신앙의 대상으로 삼는 사람은 어리석음을 면치 못 하나니라.

25. 현대과학이 아무리 만능(萬能)을 자랑하지만 자타(自他)를 위하여 순용(順用)되지 않고, 역용(逆用)되는 이상 그것은 인류에게 실리(實利)를 주는 것보다 해독(害毒)을 더 많이 주는 것이니, 다만 세계가 자타의 아상(我相)[27]이 없는 생활로 물질과 정신의 합치(合致)인 참된 과학 시대가 와야 전 인류는 합리적인 제도 하에서 안정된 생활을 하게 될 것이니, 인간의 근본을 밝히는 정신문명(精神文明)이 사람마다 마음속에 건설하여야 잘 살 수 있는 진정한 평화가 되나 니라.

---

27) 망아(妄我)에 대한 집착

26. 물질과학의 힘으로서는 자연의 일부는 정복할지언정 자연의 전체를 정복할 수는 없는 것이요, 설사 다 정복한다 하더라도 그것은 다생(多生)에 익혀 온 습성을 어느 정도까지 만족시키는 데 지나지 않을 뿐으로, 정말 습성 자체는 정복하지 못한 것이니, 그 습성 자체를 정복하고, 그 근본에 체달한 후라야 비로소 자연과 습성을 모두 자가용(自家用)으로 삼게 될 것이니라.

27. 물질과 정신이 합치된 과학자는 영원의 만능을 발휘할 수 있나 니라.

28. 현대 사람은 자만심(自慢心)을 본위로 한 신경만 예민하여, 자신이 이해 할 수 없는 법문(法門)을 들을 때에 신중히 생각하지도 아니하고, 부인할 아무 근거도 없이 무조건 반박해 버리는 것으로 쾌사(快事)를 삼는 일이 많으니, 그것은 스스로가 암흑의 길을 취하는 것이니라.

29. 아집(我執)은 배타적(排他的) 정신이라. 남이 곧 나라는 것을 알지 못하는 까닭에 나를 점점 더 축소시키는 무지이니라.

30. 중생들은 잘하고 착해야 될 줄을 알면서도, 잘하고 착하게 하는 사람, 곧 나를 찾는 공부는 할 생각을 못 하나니라.

31. 중생들은 인간이 만물(萬物) 가운데 가장 귀한 것이 사색(思索)하는데 있다고 하면서 사색하는 그 자체를 알아 볼 생각은 하지 못 하나니라.

32. 중생들은 자기 자신은 무엇인지도 까맣게 모르면서 학자인양 종교가인양 하여 제법 인생 문제를 논하는 것은 인명을

잘라 놓고 생명을 살리려는 것과 다를 바 없나 니라.

33. 이론이 끊어지고 학론(學論)이 다한 곳에서도 한 걸음 더 나아가야 나를 발견하는데, 내가 나를 찾기 전에는 인생 문제의 해결은 결코 불가능하니라.

34. 인생 문제를 해결한다는 것은 인연(행운幸運 혹은 외부 조건)이나 희망(감정적 바람)이 아니요, 진아(眞我)를 체달하여 이사(理事)에 임의로 처리하게 되어야 하나니라.

35. 중생들은 알 줄만 알고, 모를 줄은 모르 나니라.

36. 알지 못함을 알면 철저히 아는 것이니, 정말 아는 법은 알지 못할 줄을 능히 알 때에 비로소 진아(眞我)에 체달 되나 니라.

37. 지구(地球)라는 한 모태(母胎)에서 같이 출생한 동포가 서로 총칼을 겨누게 되니, 어느 형(兄)을 찌르려고 칼을 갈며, 어느 아우를 죽이려고 총을 만드는지 비참한 일이니라.

● 4. 불 법 ●

1. 불법(佛法)이라고 할 때, 벌써 불법은 아니니라.

2. 일체의 것이 그대로 불법인지라 불법이라고 따로 내세울 때에 벌써 잃어버리는 말이다.

3. 물질(物質)은 쓰는 것이요, 정신(精神)은 바탕인데, 물질과 정신의 일단화(一單化)를 불법이라 하나니라. 불법에 완전을 이루지 못하면, 인생의 영원한 전정(前程, 앞길)을 보증할 길이 없나 니라.

4. 불법은 어느 시대 어떤 인간의 호흡에도 맞는 것이니라.

5. 불법을 듣고 생명의 중심이 움직이지 않는다면, 인간의 생명을 잃어버린 사람이니라.

6. 불(佛)이라는 것은 마음이요, 법(法)이라는 것은 물질인데, 불법이라는 명상(名相)이 생기기 전에, 부처가 출현하기 전에, 나는 이미 존재한 것이니라. 질그릇 같은 나를 버리면 칠보(七寶)[28]의 그릇인 법신(法身)[29]을 얻나 니라.

7. 입이 말을 하는 것이 아니요, 손이 일을 하는 것이 아니니, 말하고 일하는 그 정체(正體)를 알아야 참된 말과 일을 하는 정작 인간(人間)이 되나 니라.

8. 불법은 육체나 영혼의 책임자이다. 책임자 없이 살아가는

---

28) 칠보 (七寶): 금, 은, 유리, 수정, 마노, 산호, 호박
29) 석가여래의 삼신(三身)의 하나로 법계(法界)의 이치와 일치한 부처의 진신(眞身).

인생이 얼마나 불안한가. 이것을 알면, 곧 불법에 돌아오게 될 것이니라.

9. 세간법(世間法)[30]과 불법이 둘이 아니요, 부처와 중생이 하나니, 이 불이법(佛二法)을 증득(證得)해야 참 인간이 되나 니라.

10. 불법을 알면 속인(俗人)이라도 스님이요, 스님이라도 불법을 모르면 이는 곧 속인이니라.

11. 여러 가지 자물쇠를 열려면 여러 가지의 열쇠가 필요한 것 같이 백 천 삼매(百千三昧)의 무량(無量)묘리(妙理)를 해득(解得)하려면 백 천만의 지혜의 열쇠를 얻어야 하나니라.

12. 불법을 부인(否認)하는 것은 자기가 자기를 부인하는 것이요, 불법을 배척하는 것은 자기가 자기를 배척하는 것이니, 이는 곧 자기가 부처이기 때문이니라.

13. 소리 소리가 다 법문(法門)이요, 두두 물물(頭頭物物)이 다 부처님의 진신(眞身)이건만, 불법 만나기는 백천만겁(百千萬劫)에 어렵다고 하니, 그 무슨 불가사의(不可思議)한 도리인지 좀 알아 볼 일이니라.

---

30) 중생들이 세상에서 쓰는 법(관습, 규칙 등 모든 것을 통칭).

● 5. 불　　교 ●

1. 불교(佛敎)라고 주장할 때 벌써 불교 교리와는 어긋난 것이니, 불교 교리는 아집(我執)[31]을 떠난 교리이기 때문이니라.

2. 불교의 종지(宗旨)는 악을 징계하고 선을 장려하는 종교가 아니다. 왜냐하면 선악이 다 불법인 까닭에 천당 극락의 즐거움이나, 반대로 지옥의 극고(極苦)한 세계가 다 나의 창조물인 까닭이니라.

3. 먼저 대가(代價)없이는 얻어지지 않고, 노력 없이는 성공이 오지 않는 것이 우주의 원리이니라.

4. 일체는 그대로 불(佛)이기 때문에 일정한 규칙이나 조직을 세워서 가르치지 않고, 기류(氣類, 근기)에 맞추어 가르칠 뿐이니라.

5. 불교의 유심(唯心)[32]이란 유물(唯物)과 상대되는 유심이 아니요, 물·심(物·心)이 둘이 아닌 절대적인 유심임을 말하는 것이니라.

6. 허공(虛空, 自我 自性)은 마음을 낳고, 마음은 인격[人格: 대표적인 인격자를 불(佛)이라함]을 낳고, 인격은 행동[현실(現實)]을 낳나 니라.

7. 세상에는 물심양면이라면 우주의 총칭(總稱)인 줄 알지만,

---

31) 망아(妄我)의 어리석음에 대한 집착.
32) 우주의 모든 존재는 마음의 표현이며, 이것을 떠나서 존재하는 것이 없고, 마음은 만물의 본체(本體)로서 유일한 실재(實在)라고 하는「화엄경」의 중심 사상.

우주의 정체(正體)는 따로 있나 니라.

8. 불교에서는 신(神)을 초월하여 법신(法身)이 있고, 영혼 위에 진인(眞人)이 있음을 알아, 그것을 증득하는 것으로 구경(究竟)을 삼는데, 육신(肉身)과 신과 영혼의 근본이 법신이요, 그 근본을 잃어버린 육신과 신과 영혼이 서로 교환 이동(移動)하는 생활이 사바세계(娑婆世界)의 인간이니라.

9. 불교는 전 인류의 자아(自我)를 완성시키는 교육 기관이니, 다종(多宗) 각법(各法)의 종교가 다 진아 완성의 가교(架橋)요 과정이니라.

10. 불교 교리의 오의(奧義)는 표현할 수 없는 법이지만, 각자가 다 이미 지니고 있기 때문에, 마음과 마음이 서로 응할 수 있고, 가르치고 가르침을 받을 수 없으되 주고받을 수 없는 그 법을 전불(前佛)[33] 후불(後佛)[34]이 상속하여 가나니라.

---

33) 현세에 나타난 부처님보다 이전에 성도(成道)하여 입멸(入滅)한 부처님.
34) 미래에 나타날 부처님 (前佛·後佛이란 중생이 모두 불성이 있으므로悉有佛性 견성하여 깨달은 부처님들의 심인心印이 면면히 상속되어 감)

● 6. 승니(僧尼)란 무엇인가? ●

1. 승(僧)이라 함은 일체 명상법(名相法)이 생기기 이전의 사람을 가리켜 승(僧)이라 하니, 만유(萬有)의 주인이요, 천상(天上) 인간의 스승이 바로 승(僧)인 것이다.

2. 수행인(修行人)인 승(僧)은 부모처자와 일체 소유를 다 버림은 물론 자신까지도 버려야 하나니라.

3. 승(僧)은 운명의 지배도 아니 받고, 염라국(閻羅國)에도 상관이 없어야 하며, 남이 주는 행•불행을 받는 사람이 되어서는 안 되나 니라.

4. 수도(修道) 생활을 하는 것은 성품(性品)이 백련(白蓮)[35]같이 되어 세속(世俗)에 물들지 않는 사람이 되려는 것이니라.

5. 짧은 일생을 위하여 세속 학문도 반평생(半平生)을 허비해야 하거든, 하물며 미래세(未來世)가 다함이 없는 전정(前程, 앞길)을 멀다 하며, 만년(萬年)을 지루하다 할 것인가?

6. 생사윤회에 소극적인 학교 교육도 필요를 느끼거든, 하물며 생사윤회를 영단(永斷)하고 참된 인간을 완성시키는 참선(參禪) 교육은 참으로 필요하다. 전 인류에게 시급히 알려야 할 가장 중요한 것이니라.

7. 세상 사람은 유위(有爲)로 법을 삼지만 승(僧)은 무위(無爲)[36]로 법을 삼나 니라.

---

35) 마음이 맑고 깨끗하여 더럽힘이 없는 것을 비유함.
36) 인연에 의하여 조작(造作)이 없는 것.

8. 세상 사람은 무엇이든지 애착심을 가지고 일을 하지만, 승(僧)은 무엇이든지 애착심을 끊고 일을 하나니, 부처님이나 조사(祖師)에게 까지도 애착심을 가지지 말 것이니라.

9. 세상에서는 혈통(血統)으로 대(代)를 이어 가지만, 승(僧)은 자기를 깨달은 정신, 곧 도(道)로 대를 이어 가는데, 세상에서도 조상의 향화(香火)[37]를 끊게 되면, 그에게 더 큰 죄가 없다는데, 불자(佛子)가 되어 승(僧)으로 부처님 법을 자기 대에 와서 끊는다면 그 죄를 어디에 비할 것인가?

10. 예전에는 항간(巷間)의 부녀자 중에도 불법을 아는 이가 있어 종종 승(僧)을 저울질하는 일이 있었건만 지금은 민중을 교화할 책임이 있는 승(僧)이 도리어 불법을 모르니, 어찌 암흑시대라 하지 않을 것이며, 시대가 이토록 캄캄한데 민중이 어찌 도탄(塗炭)에 빠지지 않을 것인가.

11. 불교의 흥망이 곧 인류의 행·불행이니라.

12. 언제나 불교의 행운과 함께 세상에 평화가 동행(同行)해 오게 되나 니라.

13. 공부하는 스님의 누더기는 임금의 용포(龍袍)로도 능히 미칠 수 없는 귀중한 것이니, 임금의 용포 밑에서는 갖은 업(業)을 짓게 되지만 중의 누더기 밑에서는 업이 녹아지고 지혜(智慧)가 밝아지나 니라.

14. 승(僧)으로서 속인의 부귀를 부러워하거나 외로워하거나 설움과 한(恨)이 남았다면 그보다 더 부끄러운 일이 없나 니라.

---

37) 제사(祭祀)

15. 이 우주 전체가 곧 '나'인 것을 깨달아 체달(體達)된 인간을 승(僧)이라 하나니라.

16. 승(僧)은 자신의 노력으로 수입되는 물질이라도 사용(私用)하지 못하나니 승(僧)의 것은 다 삼보지물(三寶之物)[38]이기 때문이니라.

17. 공부는 하지 않으면서 스님이라는 명목(名目)으로 시물(施物)을 얻어 쓰는 것은 사기취재(詐欺取財)니라.

18. 스님 노릇을 잘못하면 삼가(三家)[39]에 죄인을 면치 못하나 니라.

19. 자성(自性)이 더럽혀지기 전인 어렸을 때에 출가하여 평생을 무애(無碍)하게 스님 노릇을 잘하여 마치는 이는 하늘과 땅을 덮고도 남는 복이니라.

20. 요사이는 시주(施主)의 밥만 허비하는 스님이 많기 때문에 진실하게 공부하는 스님의 생활을 보증해 주는 신도가 없게 되었으니, 도(道)를 위하여 하는 노력은 곧 도(道)가 되나니, 도(道)를 위하여는 지악(至惡)의 경지에서도 용기 있게 노력하여 정진해야 하나니라.

21. 사상적 방향은 정진에서만 확정(確定)을 하게 되고 사상적 방향을 정하게 되어야 인생의 정로(正路)를 걷게 되고, 인생의 정로를 걷게 되어야 인생의 영원겁(永遠劫)에 장래를 보증할 수 있나 니라.

---

38) 불법승(佛法僧)을 삼보라 하고, 사찰의 공유지물(公有之物).
39) 국가, 속가(俗家), 불가(佛家).

22. 세속 일은 잠시라도 쉼이 있지만, 스님은 정진하는 일을 꿈에라도 방심(放心)할 수 없나니, 털끝만한 틈이 벌어져도 온갖 마장(魔障)이 다 생기느니라.

23. 백 천(百千) 만인(萬人)을 죽인 살인수라도 허심탄회(虛心坦懷)로 부처님께 귀의하여 정진하는 스님만 되면 백 천만인의 원결(怨結)을 푸는 동시에 백천만겁에 지은 죄업(罪業)이 몽땅 소멸 되나 니라.

24. 중생이 보고 듣고 일하는 것이 모두 허무하게 되는 것은 망아(妄我)에 집착하기 때문이니라.

25. 중생은 시공간에 의하여서만 생존하는 것으로 집착된 까닭에 시공의 제재하(制裁下)에 육도윤회를 면치 못 하나니라.

● 7. 대중 처소에서 할 행리법 ●

1. 스님은 반드시 대중(大衆)에 처(處)해야 하며, 대중을 중히 생각하여야 하나니라.

2. 스님은 당파(黨派)를 짓지 않아야 하나니, 우리라는 구분이 있다면 벌써 출가 수행자의 정신을 잃은 소리니라.

3. 출가 수행자는 물질 본위로 사는 동물적 인간계를 떠나야 할 것이니, 너와 내가 하나인 정신세계의 집단생활이 출가한 스님들의 생활이니라.

4. 대중 시봉이 곧 부처님 시봉이니라.

5. 속연(俗緣)을 끊고 출가하여 함께 정업(淨業)을 수행하는 도반(道伴)을 서로 존중히 여겨야 함을 알고, 어린이를 사랑하며, 어른에게는 공대할 줄 알아야 하느니라.

6. 이미 은사(恩師)와 상좌(上佐)의 의(義)를 맺었거든, 스승은 상좌를 지도하고, 상좌는 스승을 존경해야 하나니라.

7. 출가 수행자는 먼저 시비심(是非心)을 끊고 지내되, 남이 나를 시비할 때를 당하여 나의 잘못이 있다면 잘못을 반성하여 고치고, 만일 나의 허물이 없을 때는 나의 일이 아니니 상관치 말라. 이와 같이 대중에 처하면 불안한 시비가 없고, 항상 편안하리라.

8. 출가 수행자는 일이나 물건을 대할 때 나의 이해(利害)를 생각하지 말고, 일의 성취와 물건의 보존(保存)이 대중에게 공익으로 돌아가게 해야 하나니라.

9. 동무의 허물을 볼 때에 나의 잘못으로 느끼면 그 허물을 다른 이에게 알릴 수 없나 니라.

10. 어려운 일은 내가 하고, 좋은 음식은 남을 줄 생각을 해야 하나니라.

11. 마음은 무한대(無限大)한 것이니, 마음의 사자(使者)인 몸의 능력도 제한되지 않는 것이니라.

12. 출가 수행자는 공익(公益)심과 평등심으로 누구나 포용할 수 있어야 하나니라.

13. 출가 수행자는 곤충에게도 대자대비의 용심(用心)을 가져야 하나니라.

14. 횡재를 기뻐하지 말라. 잃어버린 임자의 슬픔이 있나 니라.

15. 출가 수행자는 먼저 인욕(忍辱)할 줄을 알아야 하나니라.

16. 대중의 욕(辱)됨을 내가 혼자 받을 마음을 가지며, 대중을 위하여서는 신명(身命)을 아끼지 않게 되어야 하나니라.

17. 대중에 처하여 각자가 자기의 임무만을 잘 충실히 지켜가면 대중 질서에 조금도 어지러운 일이 없나 니라.

18. 공적(公的) 일을 당하여 괴로움을 면할 생각을 한다든가 자기 욕심을 생각한다면 그것은 자기타락이니라.

19. 누가 내게 역량에 못 미칠 노력을 요구하더라도 원망을 말 것이니, 못 미친다는 것은 나의 정신력이 못 미친 까닭이니라.

● 8. 경 구 ●

1. 숨 한 번 마시고 내쉬지 못하면, 이 목숨은 끝나는 것이니, 이 목숨이 다하기 전에 정진력을 못 얻으면 눈빛이 땅에 떨어질 때에 내 정신이 아득하여져서 인생의 길을 잃어버리게 되나 니라.

2. 죄의 원천은 노는[40] 것이니라.

3. 자기 면목을 찾는 정진은 아니 하고 재색(財色)에 눈부터 뜨게 된다면, 천불(千佛)[41]이 출세(出世)해도 제도할 수 없나 니라.

4. 조그마한 나라를 회복하려 해도 수많은 희생을 요(要)하는 것이니, 전(全) 우주인 나를 도로 찾으려 할 때 그만한 대가를 지불할 예산을 각오해야 하나니라.

5. 누구나 물건을 잃어버린 줄은 알게 되지만, 내가 나를 잃어버린 것은 모르 나니라.

6. 미물(微物)을 업신여기는 마음으로 후일에 나도 미물이 되나 니라.

7. 남에게 이익을 주는 것이 정말 내게 이익이 되고, 남에게 베푸는 것이 정말 나에게 고리(高利)의 저금(貯金)이 되나 니라.

8. 내 잘못을 남에게 미는 것은 가장 비열한 일이니라.

---

40) 방심(放心) 해태(懈怠).
41) 과거 현재 미래의 모든 부처님.

9. 천 번 생각하는 것이 한 번 실행함만 못 하나니라.

10. 방일(放逸)은 온갖 위험을 초래하나니라.

11. 말하기 전에 실행부터 할 것이니라.

12. 총과 칼이 사람을 찌르는 것이 아니요 사람의 업(業)이 사람을 쏘고 찌르 나니라.

13. 지옥이 무서운 곳이 아니라, 내 마음 가운데 일어나는 탐(貪)진(瞋)치(痴)가 가장 무서운 것이니라.

14. 함[위(為)]이 없는 곳에 참 일이 이루어지고, 착함을 짓지 않는 곳에 정말 착함이 있나 니라.

15. 참된 말은 입 밖에 나가지 않나 니라.

16. 허공(虛空)이 가장 무서운 줄을 알아야 하느니라.

17. 네가 네 생각을 내어 놓을 수 있겠느냐?

18. 허공(虛空)이 뼈가 있는 소식을 알겠느냐?

19. 귀신 방귀에 털 나는 소식을 알겠느냐?

20. 등상불(等像佛: 나무, 돌, 쇠, 흙, 구리 등으로 만든 불상) 이 법문하는 소리를 듣겠느냐?

21. 생각이 곧 현실이요, 존재니라.

22. 생각이 있을 때는 삼라만상(森羅萬象)이 나타나고, 생각이 없어지면 그 바탕은 곧 무(無)로 돌아 가나니라.

23. 토목(土木) 와석(瓦石)이 곧 도(道)니라.

24. 백초(百草)[42]가 곧 불모[(佛母: 부처를 태어나게 하는 것, 지혜가 부처를 낳는다는 말로 반야불모(般若佛母)라는 말이 있음)]니라.

25. 부처를 풀밭[초전(草田)][43] 속에서 구할지니라.

26. 무심(無心)은 비로자나불(毘盧遮那佛)의 스승이니라.

27. 알려는 생각이 끊어질 때에 일체를 다 알게 되는 것은 무(無)에서 일체의 것이 다 발견되기 때문이니라.

28. 허수아비가 사람 못지않은 영물(靈物)임을 알아야 하나니라.

29. 얻는 것이 없으면 잃는 것도 없나 니라.

30. 유용(有用)한 인물은 한가(閑暇)한 시간을 가질 수 없나니라.

---

42) 중생의 번뇌망상, 무명초(無明草).
43) 중생의 무명(無明)을 비유함.

● 9. 최 후 설 ●

내가 산중에 와서 납자(衲子)를 가르치고 있는지 사십 (四十)여 년인데, 그 간에 선지식(善知識)을 찾아왔다 하고 나를 찾는 이가 적지 않았지만, 찾아와서는 다만 내가 사는 집인 이 육체의 모양만 보고 갔을 뿐이요, 정말 나의 진면목(眞面目)은 보지 못하였으니, 나를 못 보았다는 것이 문제가 아니라, 나를 못 보는 것이 곧 자기를 못 본 것이다. 자기를 못 봄으로 자기의 부모 형제 처자와 일체 사람을 다 보지 못하고 헛되게 돌아다니는 정신병자일 뿐이니, 이 세계를 어찌 암흑세계라 아니할 것이냐?

도(道)는 둘이 아니지만 도를 가르치는 방법은 각각 다르니, 내 법문을 들은 나의 문인(門人)들은 도절(道節)을 지켜 내가 가르치던 모든 방식까지 잊지 말고 지켜 갈지니, 도절을 지켜 가는 것이 법은(法恩)을 갚는 것도 되고, 정신적 시간적으로 공부의 손실이 없게 되나 니라.

도량(道場) 도사(道師) 도반(道伴)의 삼대 요건이 갖추어진 곳을 떠나지 말 것이니, 석가불(釋家佛) 삼천운(三千運)[44]에 덕숭산(德崇山)에서 삼성(三聖)[45]칠현(七賢)[46]이 나고, 그 외에 무수(無數) 도인(道人)이 출현할 것이니라. 나는 육체에 의존하지 아니한 영원한 존재임을 알라. 내 법문이 들리지 않을 때에도 사라지지 않는 내 면목(面目)을 볼 수 있어야 하나니라.

---

44) 석가불이 입적 하신 후 三千년.
45) 대승보살 수행의 지위인 십주(十住), 십행(十行), 십회향(十廻向) 등 세 성위(聖位)에 있는 보살. 이들은 모두 성위에 들어가기 위한 방편위(方便位)에 있는 성인(聖人)이다.
46) 대승불교에서 말하는 초발심인(初發心人), 유상행인(有相行人), 무상행인(無相行人), 방편행인(方便行人), 습종성인(習種性人), 성종성인(性種性人), 도종성인(道種性人)등 성위에 있는 현인(賢人). 칠방편(七方便), 칠가행위(七加行位)라고도 한다.

Seon Master Mangong's Dharma Talks

Preface

What is Buddhism? What kind of teaching does it truly convey? This book offers a clear and insightful answer to these timeless questions. 『Seon Master Mangong's Dharma Talks』 present the essential words of Seon Master Mangong (1872-1946), one of the great enlightened teachers of modern Korean Buddhism. Though concise, his words embody the sharp and penetrating wisdom of Seon (선, 禪) - teachings that continue to inspire practitioners across the Buddhist world. May these simple yet profound teachings awaken your heart and guide you toward the path of freedom (enlightenment).

This edition unites and refines two earlier works - the Korean 『만공 선사 법훈』 (2021) and the English 『Seon Master Mangong's Dharma Talks』. The translation has been newly revised for clarity and precision. Today, as more people in Korea and around the world visit temples and seek the meaning of Buddhist wisdom. Furthermore, an increasing number of foreigners are seeking to learn the Korean language and study Buddhism. We warmly encourage Korean readers to share this book with foreign friends and readers abroad.

Seon monk Mucho, with palms joined.

Buddhism is the path to self-perfection and a complete philosophy.

Table of Contents

❶ The Necessity of Finding Myself and Who I am

1. The meaning of humans being the noblest among all beings lies in finding and attaining "myself."

2. The meaning of "I" lies in absolute freedom. Everything should be manipulable at will. However, humans are never free, anywhere, at any time, and nothing happens as we wish. This is because the illusory self becomes the master, and the true self becomes the servant, leading our lives.

3. The illusory self is born of the true self, but the mind we currently use is the false mind. The true self is the right mind, without beginning or end, existence or non-existence, form or image, yet it is "I", lacking nothing whatsoever.

4. If a person forgets themselves, they cannot but be called humans who are no different from the six animals (육축)47). What is the difference between animals instinctively clinging to food and sex and scurrying around, and

---

47) Six common domesticated animals raised at home: cow, horse, pig, sheep, chicken, and dog.

humans who do not know their true nature and merely wander, dragged by reality? No matter how great a person may be in the world, if they do not know their true face (자기 면목), they are merely one molecule among the four births and six realms of reincarnation[48].

5. In this world where sentient beings with shared karma live, you and I live the same lives. Because of this, we live indifferently, thinking that human life is just like that. Unaware of the terrible things awaiting them, they live day by day, and when death approaches, their path ahead becomes bleak and uncertain.

6. "I" is precisely that which answers "Yes" when called someone's name. It is free from all entanglement, having no birth or death, not being burned by fire, soaked by water, or harmed by

---

48) Four Types of Birth (사생) refers to the four ways living beings come into existence: viviparous birth, oviparous birth, moisture-born birth, and transformational birth. Six Realms of Rebirth (육취) are the six destinations that sentient beings reach according to karmic causes: hell, hungry ghosts, animals, asuras (demi-gods), humans, and heavenly beings.

a knife - an independent "I."

7. Life is like a prisoner dragged and rolling, weeping, at the end of a horse's tail, pulled by the chains of karma (업), eternally traversing the path of suffering - birth, aging, sickness, and death. This iron chain can only be cut by the sword of one's own wisdom (지혜의 칼).

8. No matter how respected a person may be in society for their outstanding knowledge and character, if they do not know this matter, they have in fact lost their human spirit.

9. When Shakyamuni Buddha was born, pointing one hand to the sky and the other to the earth from his birthbed, he declared, "Above the heavens and below the heavens, only I am supremely honored." That "I" also referred to me.

10. Each individual possesses the nature to become a Buddha, but because I do not know myself, I cannot attain Buddhahood.

11. Since everything is "I," expending even the smallest bit of effort, a single hair's breadth, on

anything other than seeking this "I" is my loss.

12. Everyone possesses three bodies : the physical body, the karmic body, and the Dharma body. Only when these three bodies become one and are used as a single entity can one become a true person.

13. All actions are performed by the Dharma body, but since it is not a Dharma body separate from the physical and karmic bodies, the existing phenomena themselves are the realm of the Dharma body, which is without birth and death.

14. The realm without birth and death is possessed by both sentient and insentient beings. Therefore, not even a single blade of grass, no matter how small, can be dismantled by the entire universe's might.

15. In the world, there are words and phrases like "knowing myself" or "finding myself," but people only think of the self known through karmic consciousness (업식). They cannot even imagine what the true self is like.

16. "I" possess an infinite, immeasurable lifespan (무한 극수적 수명), an indestructible diamond body (금강불괴신) that cannot die. The life and death of this physical body are merely like changing clothes. If one is human, one should be able to freely take off and put on the clothes of life and death that one possesses.

17. It cannot be obtained through knowledge gained by seeing and hearing. Even the thought of "I" is already not "I."

18. "I" can be found in the state of no-thought (무념처), because the realm of no-thought contains all existence (일체유).

19. When one reaches the ultimate by taking Buddha as the object, it is discovered that I am precisely Buddha. Ultimately, I must discover myself within myself.

❷ How to Find Myself - Seon Meditation Method

1. In the world, there are no teachers or places that teach how to find oneself. Only in the meditation hall (선방, 禪房) within Buddhism is the sole true path to finding oneself taught.

2. Cultivating the Way (수도: 叅禪) means engaging in the practice of reclaiming one's own mind. This is an urgent matter for everyone.

3. Worldly knowledge merely serves temporary utility within the delusions of the body and then ceases. However, Seon meditation is a study that can be utilized without hindrance in any time, place, body, or life, lifetime after lifetime.

4. The meditation hall is not just a meditation hall; for those who practice Seon meditation, their own physical body is the meditation hall. Residing permanently in the meditation hall means one can practice continuously, whether walking, standing, sitting, lying down, speaking, or being silent.

5. Seon meditation absolutely cannot be done

alone. One must never depart from a Seon master (선지식), for a Seon master correctly guides one without obstruction on all matters, including the problems of life.

6. To meet a Seon master and hear even a single word of Dharma is a rare opportunity, encountered only once in tens of millions of kalpas (천만겁). If one truly understands a single word of Dharma, one can realize oneself without further meditation.

7. When listening to Dharma, one must gather one's mind with an earnest heart, as if treading on thin ice.

8. 'Seon master' is not merely a vague name like 'teacher' or 'doctor'; they are someone who has comprehended all principles and has inherited the wisdom-life of the Buddhas and patriarchs.

9. Principle (이, 理) and Phenomenon (사, 事) are the same circle. No matter from which angle one starts, if one walks without ceasing, the goal can be achieved. However, Realizing one's true self [self-realization (자각, 自覺)] is impossible

without the guidance of Seon master.

10. If one hears the Dharma talk from Seon master but dismisses it without faith and practice, one will receive the karmic retribution (과보) of not being able to hear the Dharma talk again.

11. The extent of one's practice will be accomplished in proportion to the degree of one's faith in Seon master.

12. Anyone who knows that salt is salty can practice.

13. The reason practice does not progress well is due to having idled in previous lives. One must quickly repay that debt to gain something.

14. If one has unwavering faith, the foundation of the Way is already firm.

15. To achieve success in practice, one must combine faith, determination, and doubt.

16. If faith is thorough, one's concentration (정기, 定氣) will directly justify the object, leading to autonomous accomplishment.

17. If one listens to the Dharma but their faith is not stirred, it will be difficult for them to receive a human body again in the next life.

18. The most important thing for a practitioner is to first choose a Seon master to guide them. After completing their own realization, they should then think about guiding others.

19. The greatest sin is to claim to be a Seon master and teach others without the seal of approval (인가, 印可) from an enlightened master.

20. This Dharma is a principle discovered where language is cut off and the realm of mental activity ceases (언어도단 言語道斷 심행처멸 心行處滅). It is a Dharma transmitted from mind to mind, and it cannot be learned without the direct teaching of a Seon master.

21. Since study is based on the arousal of bodhicitta - the aspiration for awakening - there are essentially no restrictions. Yet, as for the suitable age of learning, the proper time is between twenty and thirty.

22. Seon meditation is not ordinary research or study. It is a method of inquiry (참구법, 叅究法) where subject-object duality (상대, 相對) is cut off, meaning one must reach a state where not even a single hair can stir.

23. A hundred years of study is not equal to a single moment of what is obtained in the state of no-thought (무념처, 無念處).

24. All sentient beings, from birth, are accustomed to the Yin-Yang principle (음양법, 陰陽法) due to the resonance of opposite sexes. In gathering one's mind, sexual hindrance is the most powerful. Therefore, practitioners must keep the opposite sex as far away as possible.

25. One must cease all thoughts and enter into single-mindedness (일념), then go one step further from the state of no-thought, where even the thought of single-mindedness is forgotten, to discover oneself.

26. The small self (소아) must be extinguished. Therefore, before achieving success in practice, one must become like a rotten tree stump,

eradicating one's existence to the point of not caring in the slightest.

27. Three major conditions must be met to complete oneself: a place of practice (도량), a master of the Way (도사), and fellow practitioners (도반).

28. Those who follow the Way must uphold its integrity, for the Way is one. Although the methods of teaching the Way may differ slightly, failing to preserve its integrity leads to both mental and temporal loss.

29. Even for weaving a pair of straw shoes, there is a teacher, and even a famous mushroom has its growing ground. How can a person who wants to know the Way that encompasses all things become a person of the Way without the teachings of a person of the Way? And how could there not be a special ground for a person of the Way who has gathered all the right energy of the world? Furthermore, the influence of fellow practitioners (도반의 감화력) is stronger than the teacher's instruction.

30. If only the problems of life are resolved

through Seon meditation, all the various evils and sins accumulated over billions of lives and kalpas (억생 억겁) will be extinguished. At that time, one will no longer suffer in the four births and six realms49)(사생육취).

31. During cultivation of the Way, one should completely abandon living like an ordinary person, becoming like a deaf, blind, disabled person, without interfering in any other matters. Then the great self will spontaneously be realized.

32. The method of Seon meditation has existed since ancient times. In the interim, Seon masters began to teach Seon meditation through the method of raising a Hwadu, and since then, countless people of the Way (도인) have appeared. There are 1,700 Hwadus. The hwadu I first used to doubt was, "All dharmas return to one (만법 귀일); where does that one return to (일귀하처)?" This hwadu involves a dual doubt. A beginner should doubt, "All dharmas return to one, so

---

49) * Four Modes of Birth: Egg-born, Womb-born, Moisture -born, Spontaneously-born.
* Six Realms: Gods, Asuras, Humans, Animals, Hungry Ghosts, Hell-beings.

what is that one?" and continue doubting until they enter a state of calmness and clarity in no-thought, where even the thought of doubting is cut off. Only then can they see themselves.

33. The "One" is neither existence nor non-existence; it is neither spirit nor soul, nor mind. What, indeed, is this "One"? One should cultivate doubt with the same single-mindedness as a cat stalking a mouse, or as water flows without interruption. If one practices with such fervent doubt, one will surely know the "One."

34. If one claims to practice Seon meditation but still has even a slight attachment to other things, or any remaining attachment to worldly pride such as scholarship or extraordinary talents, then they are a difficult person to practice Seon. They must return to a blank slate.

35. If one undergoes severe discipline under my strictures, in return, one will obtain the great freedom of the great self.

36. In the past, there were many who instantly forgot birth and death (돈망생사) at a single word

from a Seon master, and many who saw their true nature (견성) within three or seven days at the latest. However, people nowadays have weak capacities and treat Seon meditation as a side occupation. Therefore, almost all those who have practiced for twenty or thirty years do not understand the great meaning of the Dharma.

37. Just as one must eat for oneself to feel full, if one does not practice Seon meditation for oneself, neither the Buddha nor a Seon master can save them.

38. To practice Seon meditation, one must first pacify the chaos of the six senses (the six senses: eye, ear, nose, tongue, body, and mind) and stabilize the mind. Only then is one prepared to begin practice.

39. Because this practice is the most free and simplest, those who know how to do it can even evade the eyes of the envoys of the King of Hell.

40. When one thought arises, all things are born. When one thought ceases, all things cease. The rising and ceasing of my single thought are precisely the formation and destruction (건괴)

of the universe and the birth and death of life.

41. That a word is already wrong before it leaves the mouth points to the mind before matter.

42. When one feels that their practice is going well, they have already diverged from the practice.

43. One should take what they learn and experience in dreams as a teacher.

44. When one is deeply asleep, without dreams or birth-and-death, one must know where to place their original mind (안심입명처, the state of mental peace and existential stability).

45. A dream is the action of the karmic body. When awake, one wanders with thoughts. When asleep, the karmic body manifests itself and performs the actions that the physical body performed.

46. One must be able to practice so that dream and waking (몽각) are one and the same (일여, 一如).

47. Can one maintain a normal mind when their living body is burned by fire? If one cannot

comprehend this, they must realize that when they cross the line of death (사선, 死線), their path ahead will become desolate.

48. A practitioner must practice not doing practice, but not doing practice is even more difficult than doing it.

49. More important than whether one practices well or not, one must first establish the firm faith that there is nothing else to do but this practice.

50. Whether before enlightenment (오전, 悟前) or after enlightenment (오후, 悟後), one must overcome the crisis of death at least once.

51. Seon meditation is a crucible that melts all karmic obstructions and habitual tendencies.

52. When dealing with people, one must have compassion, but for the sake of practice, if one does not have an extremely evil and poisonous mind (극악극독심), they cannot crush the eighty-four thousand afflictions (팔만사천 번뇌마).

53. Even just before an execution, there might

be lingering thoughts, but during diligent practice, not even a hair's breadth of flickering should be allowed.

54. In practice, the demon of sleep (수마, 睡魔) is more fearful than delusional thoughts (망상). One must first subdue the demon of sleep.

55. It is extremely difficult to obtain a human body. Do not miss this opportunity while you have a human body; strive diligently in your practice. If you lose this human body, it will be difficult to encounter it again.

56. When one has not gained strength in practice, at the moment of death (안광낙지, 眼光落地) only human karma remains. In this state, even animals may appear as handsome men or beautiful women, and it becomes easy to be ensnared within their wombs.

57. The time of a Seon practitioner is extremely precious. One must not waste even a moment.

58. There is no time as free and leisurely as the time spent sitting in the toilet. If one can

enter into single-mindedness (일념) even then, one can see one's true nature (견성).

59. The reason practice is delayed is always because there is a lingering thought of having time to spare and constantly postponing it. One must encourage oneself every day, saying, "I woke up today and am still alive, so I must complete my practice today. How can I trust tomorrow?"

60. When lying down at night, one should review the day's practice. If more time was spent on delusional thoughts and drowsiness than on diligent practice, one should gather great courage again and practice diligently, doing so consistently every day.

61. If one feels drowsy or has delusional thoughts during practice, one should re-examine their own future, realizing they are not free from the great matter of birth and death. Then their mind will spontaneously refresh.

62. When crossing the line of death, if there is even a hair's breadth of selfishness (사심) left, even the memory of practicing Seon will vanish.

63. One becomes a monk by leaving home to escape the cycle of birth and death. Any activity performed apart from Seon meditation is merely cultivating the Dharma of birth and death.

64. If one practices Seon meditation with the mind of seeking the Way, believing that the Way exists separately, one will fall into heterodoxy (외도).

65. Even if a person of the Way performs all sorts of miraculous powers, and even at the time of death shows incredible and wondrous signs, these are all phenomenal dharmas (상법, 相法), and none of them are worth clinging to.

66. Faith is the stepping stone to ascending and finding the Buddha. Therefore, one must step on the foundation of egoless faith, transcend the Buddha, and find one's own true essence.

67. A Seon practitioner must conduct themselves with solemnity, so that they can teach others even without opening their mouths.

68. The path of practice has four stages: knowing no birth and death (지무생사, 知無生死), harmonizing

with no birth and death (계무생사, 契無生死), embodying no birth and death (체무생사, 體無生死), and using no birth and death (용무생사, 用無生死). Only upon reaching the stage of using no birth and death does one truly become a greatly free person, unhindered in principle (이무애) and unhindered in phenomena (사무애).

69. When practicing, do not intentionally try to know. If you gain the power of diligent practice, enlightenment will naturally be achieved.

70. If, before completion of practice, one thinks they have already realized something and becomes lazy, they are likely to lose even their Buddhist affinity.

71. The mind, which does not depend on matter, can actualize all actions from a state of formlessness.

72. Mind is the creator of matter, but without matter, the existence and effect of mind cannot be manifested.

73. Matter only performs one responsibility according to its name, but the mind, though without

name or form, is the fundamental essence of all things. It is an absolute capable agent in any situation or task. Everyone possesses this mind. If one only rediscovers this mind, they will become an all-capable person.

74. Within the temple of the mind, the two actors of birth and death, good and evil, take turns performing infinite forms of comedies and tragedies against the backdrop of the myriad phenomena.

75. No matter how civilized a country may be, if it lacks a person of the Way, it is an empty country. No matter how poor a country may be, if it has even one person of the Way, that country is not empty.

76. A person of the Way (도인, 道人) should not be a person of the Way who is merely a generic term for a person of the Way. One must realize the message before names and forms arise, leave behind the idol of being a person of the Way, and break free from the constraints of precepts and cultivation to become a completely independent human being. Only then can one traverse the six realms and be free from suffering.

❸ On Present Life

1. Human life is but a brief act in a play. When one scene of this play ends, the consciousness that performed joy, sorrow, anger, and pleasure disappears without a trace, and the body decays. How fleeting this is! And during this utterly fleeting period, was there even a moment of freedom? If unexpected death strikes while eating, one must die without even swallowing the chewed rice. If one builds a splendid house with much money, only to encounter a sudden fire, they may not even get to sit in it once before it all becomes futile. If I constantly lose freedom even in my own affairs, how sorrowful is the endeavor of building a society and nation, which are collections of human lives? Should one not obtain the foundation of freedom to achieve fundamental freedom? Humans who do not even know where freedom is obtained, yet shout for freedom, are like talking about cooking rice and eating it to satiety without any rice.

2. Human life is a dream-like illusion, a reflection of one's karmic body, which they mistake for reality, leading to weeping and laughter. This is

like a ginkgo tree producing fruit by resonating with its own reflection in the water, which it mistakes for the opposite sex.

3. Human existence is not a continuous sequence of life, but a continuous sequence of birth and death (생멸). Humans, at the moment of death, forget their lives before and after death, and do not remember the suffering of entering and exiting the womb (입태·출태). They only perceive this life that can be judged by the six consciousnesses (육식, 六識). Such a life, where one goes to heaven, then to hell, becomes a human, then falls into an animal form, passes quickly, and another life quickly approaches, is like the continuous exchange and movement of images in a movie, appearing as different scenes in a rapid moment.

4. Life cannot recall the past nor guarantee the future. Because the present is the present, one must fully grasp the present to live a life where past, present, and future are unified into one.

5. Life does not live in the past, nor in the future, but only in the present. The present is a moment that ceaselessly moves from past to

future. How can such an unstable life be called real? There is a reality where past and present are united, for the present is the successor of the past and the precursor of the future, as past, present, and future are one.

6. Centering on the world we live in, there are countless unimaginable supreme cultural worlds spread above, and below, an immeasurable number of low-level and extremely evil hellish worlds, all of which are dream-like worlds. What, then, is the true world? To know and attain that is to realize the world of the true self (진아세계).

7. My current life is the entire world. If I cannot find self-sufficiency (자족, 自足) in my current life, there is no way to find it again.

8. Humans all hope for good things to come to them and continue their lives, but they do not know that taking good things is precisely the cause of obtaining unpleasant things.

9. One must clearly realize that the main elements of human life - birth, aging, sickness, death (생로병사) and joy, anger, sorrow, pleasure

(희로애락) - are all accumulations and results of deluded habits cultivated over many lives. Only then can one escape birth and death.

10. This universe is filled with an infinite, immeasurable number of different kinds of sentient beings, each establishing a living environment suited to their habits. However, our six consciousnesses have become increasingly fixated due to habitual tendencies from many lives. Therefore, as humans in this Saha World, we cannot possibly see or feel beyond a certain limit. Heavenly beings, hellish beings, gods, and ghosts are ultimately just names and forms of different kinds of sentient beings that our six consciousnesses cannot judge.

11. Habit is second nature. So-called genius and talent are also things that have been cultivated and fixed over many lives. This is precisely what karma (업, 業) is.

12. Matter undergoes a dual action of combination (결합) and dissolution (해소). Therefore, the universe is built and destroyed, and life repeats birth and death eternally.

13. Sentient beings are those who live a small-self (소아) existence confined to a single entity, such as humans, animals, and insects, having lost all freedom and merely wandering through the four births and six realms (사생육취), driven by the winds of karma (업풍). A Buddha, or an enlightened person, is one who has self-actualized the entire universe, seeing all sentient beings as one's own body and the three thousand great thousand worlds as one's own home. They can take and discard any home or body at will.

14. An enlightened person (완인, 完人) has self-actualized all things (만유를 자체화); therefore, they can freely create the forms of all things and freely use the principles of all things.

15. Ordinary beings say that heaven is a place to go, and hell is a place never to go. Yet the universe is but my one body, and heaven and hell are but my one home. Deluded beings divide this single world into two realms, splitting their own one body and sending it separately to heaven and hell. This, indeed, arises from the karmic conditions (업연. 業緣) of sentient beings.

16. A person whose character is swayed by circumstances will never find eternal peace.

17. Worldly people take bags of dung and blood as their bodies and value only cold, heat, thirst, and hunger. Therefore, they can never escape the bitter suffering of samsara.

18. The six consciousnesses - eye, ear, nose, tongue, body, and mind consciousness - that we experience change according to place and scatter according to time. How can human beings grasp the fundamental spirit with these six consciousnesses that constantly shift from moment to moment?

19. No matter how advanced the theories or profound the doctrines of worldly people may be, they cannot possibly solve the problems of life. This is because they are attached to names and forms (명상, 名相).

20. If a theory clearly enlightens what cannot be solved by theory, then that theory becomes a great guide leading one to the entrance of the Way.

21. Those who speak of metaphysics or idealism

do not know that they themselves have not escaped the material realm.

22. For the awakened, there is no one who speaks truly right, nor anyone who speaks truly wrong, for all dualistic notions have ceased.

23. A god, no matter how supremely mighty or miraculously free, even if believed to control human fate and fortune, lacking a physical body, remains a 'deviant' entity.

24. Those who deny divine being cannot escape ignorance, and those who make divine being an object of faith cannot escape foolishness.

25. No matter how much modern science boasts of its omnipotence, if it is not used for the benefit of oneself and others, but rather misused, it brings more harm than benefit to humanity. Only when the world enters a true age of science, where material and spiritual are united, without the ego-clinging (아상, 我相) of oneself and others, will all humanity live a stable life under a rational system. True peace, where people can live well, will come only when a spiritual civilization that

illuminates the foundation of humanity is built in each person's heart.

26. The power of material science can conquer a part of nature, but not the whole of nature. Even if it were to conquer all of nature, it would merely satisfy one's habitual tendencies cultivated over many lives to some extent. It would not truly conquer the habits themselves. Only after conquering the habits themselves and realizing their root can one finally make both nature and habits their own.

27. A scientist who has unified matter and spirit can display eternal omnipotence.

28. Modern people are hypersensitive, primarily driven by arrogance. When they hear Dharma that they cannot understand, they often take pleasure in unconditionally refuting it without careful thought or any basis for denial. This is choosing the path of darkness for themselves.

29. Self-clinging (아집, 我執) is an exclusive mind. It is the ignorance of not knowing that others are precisely oneself, and thus it increasingly

shrinks oneself.

30. Though sentient beings know they ought to be good and virtuous, they neglect to undertake the practice of seeking that which makes one good and virtuous - the true self.

31. Sentient beings claim that humans are the most precious of all beings because they can think, yet they do not think about how the act of thinking itself arises

32. Sentient beings, completely unaware of what they themselves are, yet discussing the problems of life as if they were scholars or religious figures, is no different from cutting off a person's life and trying to save their life.

33. One must go one step further even where theories are cut off and academic arguments cease to discover oneself. Before I find myself, the solution to the problems of life is absolutely impossible.

34. To solve the problems of life is not a matter of luck, external conditions, or emotional hopes,

but of realizing the True Self (진아, 眞我), so that one may freely and wisely respond to both principle and phenomena.

35. Sentient beings only know how to know; they do not know how to not know.

36. If one knows that they do not know, then they know thoroughly. The true way of knowing is only when one can truly know what it means not to know; then one finally realizes the true self.

37. It is tragic that compatriots, born from the same womb of Earth, point guns and knives at each other. Which brother are they sharpening their knives for, and which younger sibling are they making guns to kill?

❹ Dharma

1. When one speaks of Dharma, it is already not Dharma.

2. Everything itself is Dharma. To set Dharma apart as something separate is already to lose it.

3. Matter is for use, and mind is the ground. The unification of matter and mind is called Dharma. If one does not achieve perfection in Dharma, there is no way to guarantee the eternal future of life.

4. Dharma is suitable for the breath of any human being in any era.

5. If one hears the Dharma and the core of their being is not stirred, they are one who has lost their human life

6. Buddha refers to the mind, and Dharma refers to matter. Before the name and form of Dharma arose, and before the Buddha appeared, I already existed. If one casts aside this self, which is like a clay vessel, one attains the Dharma Body,

a vessel of the seven treasures (Gold, Silver, Lapis Lazuli, Crystal, Agate, Coral, and Amber).

7. The mouth does not speak, nor do hands work. One must know the true essence that speaks and works to become a true human being who speaks and works genuinely.

8. Dharma is responsible for the physical body and the soul. How insecure is a life lived without a responsible entity? Knowing this will immediately bring one back to the Dharma.

9. Worldly phenomena and Dharma are not two, and Buddha and sentient beings are one. One must realize this non-dual Dharma to become a true human being.

10. If one understands the Dharma, even a layperson is a monk; if a monk does not understand the Dharma, they are a layperson.

11. Just as various keys are needed to open various locks, one must obtain countless keys of wisdom to understand the immeasurable subtle principles of hundreds and thousands of

samadhis.

12. To deny the Dharma is to deny oneself. To reject the Dharma is to reject oneself, for one is precisely the Buddha.

13. Every sound is Dharma, and every single thing is the Buddha's true body. Yet, it is said that encountering the Dharma is difficult in hundreds of millions of kalpas. What an inconceivable principle this is, one should truly try to understand it.

❺ Buddhism

1. When one asserts "Buddhism," it already contradicts Buddhist doctrine, because Buddhist doctrine is a doctrine that has abandoned self-clinging (아집, 我執).

2. The ultimate principle of Buddhism is not a religion that punishes evil and promotes good. This is because both good and evil are, in their very essence, the Dharma. Consequently, the pleasures of heaven or nirvana, and conversely, the extreme suffering of hell, are all creations of my own mind.

3. Nothing is gained without a price, and success does not come without effort. This is the principle of the universe.

4. Everything is inherently Buddha. Therefore, it is not taught with fixed rules or organizations, but merely taught according to the aptitude of the individual.

5. The "Mind-Only" (유심, 唯心) of Buddhism is not a mind-only that is relative to materialism; it

refers to an absolute mind-only where mind and matter are not two.

6. Emptiness (Self-nature) gives birth to mind, mind gives birth to character (The quintessential embodiment of such character is called a Buddha), and character gives birth to action.

7. In the world, people think of mind and matter as the totality of the universe, but the true nature of the universe exists separately.

8. Buddhism understands that there is a Dharma Body beyond God and a True Person beyond the soul. To realize these is the ultimate goal. The Dharma Body is the root of the physical body, God, and the soul. Humans in the Saha world live a life where these physical body, God, and soul, having lost their root, are constantly exchanging and moving.

9. Buddhism is an educational institution that perfects the self of all humanity. All various sects and methods of religion are bridges and processes for the completion of the true self.

10. The profound meaning of Buddhist doctrine is a Dharma that cannot be expressed, but because each person already possesses it, mind can resonate with mind. Although it cannot be taught or received, it is transmitted from previous Buddhas to future Buddhas.

➏ What is Sunim?

1. By 'Sunim' (스님, 僧) is meant the one who existed before all concepts and phenomena arose. It is this Sunim who is the master of all existence and the teacher of both heavenly beings and humans."

2. A practitioner who is a Sunim must abandon not only parents, spouse, children, and all possessions but also their very self.

3. A Sunim should not be subject to the dictates of fate, should have no connection to The netherworld, and should not be a person who receives happiness or misfortune from others.

4. Living a life of cultivation means becoming a person whose nature is like a white lotus, unstained by worldly affairs.

5. If one must spend half their life on worldly studies for a short lifespan, why should one complain that the endless future life is long or that ten thousand years is tedious?

6. If even school education, which is passive in the cycle of birth and death, is considered necessary, how much more essential is Seon meditation education, which permanently cuts off the cycle of birth and death and completes the true human being? This is the most important thing that needs to be urgently communicated to all humanity.

7. Worldly people take conditioned phenomena as their Dharma, but Sunim take unconditioned phenomena as their Dharma.

8. Worldly people do things with attachment, but Sunim does things by cutting off attachment. Sunim should not even have attachment to the Buddha or the Patriarchs.

9. In the world, generations are continued through bloodlines, but Sunims continue their lineage through their realized mind, that is, the Way. In the world, it is said that there is no greater sin than to cut off the ancestral rites (조상 제례). If a Buddhist disciple, as a Sunim, cuts off the Buddha's Dharma in their own generation, what sin could compare to that?

10. In the past, even laywomen in the common streets knew the Dharma and often weighed the worth of Sunims. But now, Sunims, who are responsible for teaching the public, are ignorant of the Dharma. How can we not call this a dark age? And if the age is so dark, how can the people not fall into misery?

11. The rise and fall of Buddhism are directly linked to the happiness and misfortune of humanity.

12. Peace in the world always accompanies the good fortune of Buddhism.

13. The patched robe of a practicing Sunim is more precious than an emperor's imperial robe. Under an emperor's robe, various karmas are created, but under a Sunim's robe, karma melts away and wisdom brightens.

14. If a Sunim envies the wealth and honor of laypeople, feels lonely, or harbors sorrow and resentment, there is no greater shame than that.

15. A person who realizes and embodies that this entire universe is "I" is called a Sunim.

16. A Sunim cannot use even material goods obtained through their own efforts for personal use, because everything belonging to a Sunim is property of the Three Jewels.

17. To obtain and use offerings under the name of a Sunim without doing any practice is fraud.

18. If a Sunim performs their duties poorly, they cannot escape being a sinner to the three families (the State · the Lay Society · Sangha / 국가 · 속가 · 불가 /   國家 · 俗家 · 佛家).

19. One who leaves home at a young age, before their nature is defiled, and perfectly fulfills the role of a Sunim throughout their life, unhindered, has accumulated merit that covers heaven and earth.

20. These days, there are many Sunims who only consume the offerings of laypeople, so there are no longer lay supporters who guarantee the livelihood of truly practicing Sunims. Effort

made for the Way becomes the Way itself. For the sake of the Way, one must bravely strive and practice even in the most evil circumstances.

21. Ideological direction is only confirmed through diligent practice. Only when ideological direction is established can one walk the right path of life, and only by walking the right path of life can one guarantee the future throughout eternal kalpas.

22. Worldly affairs have moments of rest, but a Sunim cannot relax from diligent practice even in dreams. If there is even a hair's breadth of laxity, all kinds of demonic obstacles will arise.

23. Even a murderer who has killed hundreds of thousands of people, if they return to the Buddha with an open and honest heart and practice diligently as a Sunim, they will resolve the resentment of hundreds of thousands of people and simultaneously extinguish all the karmic sins accumulated over hundreds of millions of kalpas.

24. The reason sentient beings' seeing, hearing,

and working all become futile is because they cling to the illusory self (망아, 忘我).

25. Sentient beings are attached to existing only in time and space; therefore, they cannot escape the six paths of reincarnation (육도윤회, 六道輪廻) under the constraints of time and space.

❼ Conduct in the Sangha

1. A Sunim must reside among the community and regard the community as important.

2. A Sunim should not form factions. If there is a distinction of "us," then one has already lost the spirit of a renunciant practitioner.

3. A renunciant practitioner must abandon the animalistic human realm that lives primarily for material things. The communal life of renunciant Sunim is a spiritual world where you and I are one.

4. Serving the Sangha is precisely serving the Buddha.

5. Having cut off worldly ties and left home to practice the pure path together, one must respect fellow practitioners, love children, and show reverence to elders.

6. Once the relationship of master and disciple (은사 상좌, 恩師 上座) has been formed, the master must guide the disciple, and the disciple must respect the master.

7. A renunciant practitioner must first cut off the mind of right and wrong. When others criticize them, if there is a fault, they should reflect on and correct it. If there is no fault, it is not their concern, so they should not interfere. If one conducts themselves in this way within the community, there will be no uneasy disputes and they will always be at peace.

8. When a renunciant practitioner deals with tasks or objects, they should not think of their own gain or loss, but rather ensure that the completion of the task and the preservation of the object benefit the community.

9. When seeing the faults of a companion, if one feels it as their own fault, they cannot reveal that fault to others.

10. One should think, "I will take on the difficult tasks myself, and let others have the good food."

11. The mind is infinite; therefore, the ability of the body, which is the mind's messenger, is also unlimited.

12. A renunciant practitioner must be able to em-

brace everyone with a public spirit and equanimity.

13. A renunciant practitioner must have a mind of great compassion even towards insects.

14. Do not rejoice in unexpected gains. There is the sorrow of the owner who lost it.

15. A renunciant practitioner must first learn to forbear.

16. One should have the mind to endure the disgrace of the community alone and not spare one's life for the community.

17. If each individual in the community faithfully performs their own duties, there will be no disorder in the community's order.

18. If one tries to avoid suffering or thinks of their own desires when performing public duties, it is their own degradation.

19. Even if someone demands an effort beyond your capacity, do not resent it, for your mental power is insufficient.

⑧ Sayings

1. If one cannot exhale after inhaling once, this life ends. If one does not gain the power of diligent practice before this life ends, when their eyesight falls to the ground, their mind will become distant, and they will lose the path of life.

2. The source of sin is idleness.

3. If one does not diligently seek their true face but instead opens their eyes to wealth and sex, even a thousand Buddhas appearing in the world cannot save them.

4. Even to restore a small country requires numerous sacrifices. When seeking to regain the entire universe, which is myself, one must be prepared to pay that much.

5. Everyone knows when they lose an object, but they do not know that they have lost themselves.

6. By despising a tiny creature, I will become a tiny creature in the future.

7. Giving benefit to others truly benefits me, and giving to others truly becomes high-interest savings for me.

8. Pushing my fault onto others is the most contemptible act.

9. A thousand thoughts are worth less than one action.

10. Indulgence brings forth all kinds of dangers.

11. Act before you speak.

12. Guns and knives do not pierce people; a person's karma shoots and pierces them.

13. Hell is not a frightening place; the greed, anger, and ignorance that arise in my mind are the most frightening.

14. True work is accomplished where there is no doing, and true goodness exists where no goodness is performed.

15. True words do not leave the mouth.

16. One must know that emptiness is the most terrifying thing.

17. Can you put forth your own thoughts?

18. Do you know the message of emptiness having bones?

19. Do you know the message of hair growing on a ghost's fart?

20. Can you hear a Buddha statue speaking the Dharma?

21. Thought is precisely reality and existence.

22. When there is thought, all phenomena appear, and when thought ceases, its essence returns to nothingness.

23. Earth, wood, tiles, and stones are precisely the Way.

24. All plants are precisely the Buddha-mother (Prajñāpāramitā is called the Mother of all Buddhas, because through wisdom, all Buddhas

are born).

25. Seek the Buddha in the grass field[50].

26. No-mind is the teacher of Vairocana Buddha.

27. When the thought of knowing ceases, one knows everything, because everything is discovered from nothingness .

28. One must know that a scarecrow is a spiritual being no less significant than a human.

29. If there is nothing to gain, there is nothing to lose.

30. A useful person cannot have idle time.

---

50) The grass field symbolizes the ignorance of sentient beings.

❾ Last Words

I have been in the mountains, teaching practitioners for over forty years. During that time, not a few came seeking a Seon master, seeking me. But they only saw the shape of this physical body, the house where I live, and did not see my true face. The problem is not that they could not see me, but that not seeing me is precisely not seeing themselves. By not seeing themselves, they are merely psychiatric patients wandering aimlessly, unable to see their parents, siblings, spouse, or any other person. How can this world not be called a dark world?

The Way is not two, but the methods of teaching the Way differ. My disciples who have heard my Dharma talks must uphold the discipline of the Way and not forget all the methods I taught. Upholding the discipline of the Way repays the Dharma's grace (법은, 法恩) and prevents spiritual and temporal loss in practice.

Do not leave the place where the three great requirements of practice ground (도량, 道場), master (도사, 道師), and fellow practitioners (도반, 道伴) are met. In the 3,000 cycles of

Shakyamuni Buddha, three sages and seven worthies will emerge from Deokseung-san (덕숭산), and countless other people of the Way (도인, 道人) will appear. Know that I am an eternal being, not dependent on the physical body. Even when my Dharma talks are no longer heard, you must be able to see my true face, which does not vanish.

- End -